JOSEPHINE:
THE MOUSE SINGER

ALSO BY MICHAEL McCLURE

The Adept
Antechamber & Other Poems
The Beard
Dark Brown
Gargoyle Cartoons
Ghost Tantras
Gorf
Hymns to St. Geryon
Jaguar Skies
Little Odes
The Mad Cub
Meat Science Essays
The New Book / A Book of Torture
Passage
Rare Angel
September Blackberries
Star

JOSEPHINE: THE MOUSE SINGER
Michael McClure

Preface by Michael Feingold

A NEW DIRECTIONS BOOK

Manufactured in the United States of America
First published as New Directions Paperbook 496 in 1980
Published simultaneously in Canada by George McLeod, Ltd., Toronto

Library of Congress Cataloging in Publication Data
McClure, Michael.
    Josephine: the mouse singer.
    (A New Directions Book)
    I. Title.
PS3563.A262J6   812'.5'4   79–25429
ISBN 0–8112–0755–2

New Directions Books are published for James Laughlin
by New Directions Publishing Corporation,
80 Eighth Avenue, New York 10011

PREFACE

All beasts are human—and vice versa, of course—but none more so than the mouse. The monkey looks so much like us that we automatically note his differences from us in self-defense. The larger mammals are a threat, or a source of meat, or our competitors for it. Birds have capacities that we envy—plumage, flight, song—and insects are too small to enforce the resemblance on our minds, while reptiles tend to remind us of our unpleasant side. House cats have a secret aspect that keeps them remote from us, and fish have their mysterious underwater complacency. At best, most of these creatures are only good for a simile or two in our minds: we can drink like a fish, keep busy as a bee or a beaver, screech like a jackdaw, be dumb as an ox or sly as a fox or stubborn as a donkey or shy as a giraffe or hung like a horse (or drunk as a skunk, though this image is really based on rhyme and unfair to the animal in question). We can go to the ant or weep crocodile tears or hump like rabbits or jabber like monkeys; we can insult someone by calling him a dirty rat, a louse, a dodo, a snake in the grass, a toad, a chicken, a stupid cow, a horse's ass. You will note that all of these comparisons have their opprobrious side; we don't really like to think about how close we are to the animals, which is why artists have to keep reminding us of the relationship: mere lumps of meat and water like us don't have any right to put on airs of superiority.

The mouse is a great friend to artists, then, because we can like him. He doesn't seem to have any specially bad characteristics—at worst, his life is a little drab, but we all suspect our lives of being just that. A mouse will bite, but only when attacked (unlike rats, who don't need provocation); he may frighten women a little as he scampers by, but his own fright and eagerness to escape are so evident that we can hardly hold that against him. Not enough like us to unnerve us, he is a tiny creature (therefore clearly inferior) who looks up to us and fears us (therefore reassuring), who is not directly useful to us (therefore not a menial), and can be a pleasant furry companion without making extensive demands on us (therefore a true friend). No wonder artists appreciate the mouse; put him in a work and you win your human audience instantly. Nothing pains us more in *Alice in Wonderland* than Alice being rude to the sad little mouse in the Pool of Tears; nothing in the acidulous chill of Edward Albee's work is more humanizing than the image of Martha's late father, in *Virginia Woolf,* as a little white mouse with tiny red eyes. You probably think Prince Hamlet called *The Murder of Gonzago* "the mousetrap" because he was planning to "catch the conscience of the king" in it; not so. He was actually planning to show how Claudius (the rat—remember "Help, ho! A rat!") caught Gertrude:

> Let the bloat king tempt you again to bed,
> Pinch wanton on your cheek, *call you his mouse,* &c.

My italics, but Shakespeare's image. That poor put-upon Queen of Denmark is the mouse in question; her late husband, if you remember, Hamlet addresses as "old mole." Something is rodent in the state of Denmark, and it's human beings. Shakespeare clearly saw no shame in the comparison.

Now about Michael McClure's mice. They are nothing new for him. You might say, in fact, that for all the differences between the two writers, Kafka's parable comes made to order for the poet who sketched Minnie Mouse's encounter with the tap-dancing Buddha in an earlier play. Mice, as I have been pointing out, are ideal subjects to a writer who celebrates the animal side of humanity, and even its plant connections. ("Let's give the redwoods the vote!" a McClure character once shouted.) And the mouse-world, it turns out, is an ideal place for Kafka's vision of the universe and Mc-Clure's to collide and merge into one. Kafka used many animal metaphors as a way of denigrating humanity: poor

Gregor Samsa, who let down the biped side by metamorphosing into a cockroach. Or the mangy, servile mutts of *Forschungen eines Hundes,* always ready to deny the Invisible Hand that feeds them reasons for existing. This animal world of ours, full of uncontrollable instincts, set in a universe of terror and arbitrariness, was a source of horrified fascination for Kafka. For McClure, it's something to be celebrated, the joy of uncertainty, the notion that in the music of the spheres, any chord may suddenly resolve into another on the big harmonium. But the seething chaos, whether looked at from its good side or its bad, is still a chaos, still seething.

This reversibility of vision is a paradox, a thing that makes sense without being explicable. Kafka's nightmare view of life turns out to contain an ecstatic joy, just as the drab existence of the mice contains Josephine's transfiguring music. McClure's vision, which celebrates the ecstasy, turns out to celebrate the nightmare as well: Josephine's exhaustion, her frustration, her virtually feminist bitterness when mouse-males treat her as a mere love object, become part of the Josephine myth (McClure, dissatisfied with Kafka's blunt naturalistic conclusion, has made sure that the story turns into a myth). Josephine's story is a song of praise to the meatness and waterness of our existence, as well as to the invisible music that transfigures it, so wonderfully summed up in Josephine's piped songs, concrete expressions of the inexpressible. At the same time, this song of praise is a satire, which always means a shriek of pain, on our innate gift for being deaf to the transfiguring song. Or for instantly dismissing it as a copy of something else, mere folk-piping which anyone could do as well as Josephine. That's the beauty of the mouse image: in the shadow of great art, we are all mice; even the artist is a tiny being next to the greatness created out of his/her blood and bone. We may feel taken down a peg, but our miceness has a niceness to it, a sense of security threatened by only one thing: art. And the artist, who knows this threat better than anyone else, shares with every other artist the joy of living on the edge of the threat, while the rest of us occasionally tiptoe up and sniff at it, like mice at the cheese in a trap. That's why a parable of Kafka's can become a play of McClure's with no stylistic discrepancy intervening: Kafka's long, elaborate sentences, laid out in polished clauses like the corridors of a palace, tend to lead nowhere, or at best to sinkholes and contradictions. (One of his most perfect short pieces, *Auf der Galerie,* consists of two thick paragraphs, each one sentence long, that perfectly contradict each other.) For German readers, Kafka's is the language that gives the lie to language, the syntax that denies the utility of syntax. And what else is McClure doing when he throws away grammar, and even words, and writes in growls and snarls and pipes instead? Giving the lie to language, in an American rather than a German way. Every writer knows that the point of what you express is the inexpressible; the words are only the vehicle that gets you to that point. Which seems precisely the spot where the critic should stop introducing you to the playwright, and let his characters, who will do a much better job, take over. They, after all, can pipe at will, while I have to pretend to rational discourse. If this seems unfair, I can always remind myself that I am a man, while they are mice, and I can always pretend to have gotten the better part of the deal—until the next time McClure's art starts messing up my head.

MICHAEL FEINGOLD

The first production of *Josephine: The Mouse Singer,* directed by Gerry Woodard, opened at the WPA Theatre in New York on November 30, 1978. The costumes were designed by David Menkes, with set and lighting by Craig Evans. The actors performed multiple roles, except for the Narrator, Josephine, and Baby.

NARRATOR	WILLIAM VERDERBER
BABY	MICHAEL FRENCH
JOSEPHINE	GALE GARNETT

The other players were: Sanford Morris, Dan Bonnell, Janice Kay Young, Nancy Parent, Vicki Hirsch, David Hall, Mary Diveny, Brian Carpenter, and Larry Dilg.

Josephine: The Mouse Singer had its West Coast premier on October 5, 1979, with the Magic Theatre at Fort Mason, San Francisco. It was directed by John Lion, with costumes by Regina Cate, scenic design by Don Cate, and lighting by Anne E. Militello.

NARRATOR	MATTHEW LOCRICCHIO
BABY	ED KASKY
JOSEPHINE	SIGRID WURSCHMIDT

The other players were: Luc Alexander, Vivian Altmann, Kathleen Amorose, John J. Finch, Tom Fleming, Michael Grodenchik, Julie Jay, Francine Lembi, Roxanne Rogers, and Dan St. Paul.

All characters are mice, with mouse ears and tails.

They are dressed in Edwardian and Victorian costumes. Some men mice wear spats and tennis shoes. Some females wear a sunbonnet and carry an umbrella, parasol, or muff.

The mice appear in wigs, bowler hats, top hats, workmen's clothes, mustaches. There is an indeterminate number of mice.

There are minimal sets. Action occurs in spotlights or pools of light on the otherwise dark stage. When a mouse is not in the light then he is out of the action and does not bother to leave the stage.

There is the ringing of a hand bell in blackness. A circle of light comes up on the Narrator. He stands on a large rock surrounded by oversized straw and is ringing a bell. The Narrator is dressed in Victorian style. He has mouse ears and tail.

NARRATOR [*finishes ringing bell*]:
>Josephine's our singer. She has the power
>of song! And if you hear her
>—if anyone does—then they become
>delirious—either all sighs
>or solemn silence . . .

[*Mouse One steps into the light.*]

MOUSE ONE [*dressed in a hat and big handlebar mustache*]:
>Hey! We're not a music-loving tribe!

1

NARRATOR:
Well, all the more tribute to her
—that we gather in huge crowds to listen.

MOUSE ONE:
Mostly we love plain silence.

NARRATOR:
Then, that's still more in her honor.
We live in quiet in our hardworking, mousely
cunning as we move
in dimensions of darkened corners.

MOUSE ONE:
Yeah, that's right.
As much as we adore silence, to love Josephine's
singing is something.

[*He tips his hat.*]

See you!
[*He exits.*]

NARRATOR [*solo*]:
Music has never been important to us
Nor have we yearned for it.
Nor have we missed it in its
absence. Before Josephine there
never was a singer—no one who
made serious songs among all our people.
Our tribe was bare of her pure
love of music and
her voice . . .

[*Mouse Two steps into the light.*]

MOUSE TWO [*He wears a long wig and is biting a cigar. He
carries a huge head of wheat. He doffs his bowler hat*]:
That's right!

2

                    No one before
                    her sang.

NARRATOR:
                It is the perfect beauty of her voice
                      that fills all and any
                    ears from the subtle
                 to the most insensitive.

MOUSE TWO:
                    That's true. I pride myself
                    on my ear's insensitivity
                    but I'll stand barefoot
                    in the snow to hear her.

[*Brief pause*]

                    Must run. See you.

[*He shakes the head of wheat, which rattles, and exits.*]

NARRATOR [*solo*]:
                Though one would expect something special
                    from what is called singing
                       that's not the case
                     with Josephine . . .

[*Mouse Three steps into the light.*]

MOUSE THREE [*wears a long white beard*]:

                    That's right, brother.

NARRATOR:
                      In fact, we are taken
                 as we listen—and we often
                    speak about this . . .

[*Mouse Four steps into the light.*]

                            3

MOUSE FOUR [*a very fat mouse carrying an enormous piece of Swiss cheese*]:
> I.e., that nothing extraordinary is
> in Josephine's singing. It
> is capable of calling
> the most profound attention
> from us—our deepest attention . . .

NARRATOR:
> But we freely admit that there
> is nothing out of the ordinary
> about it.

MOUSE FOUR:
> Must run, old chop.

[*He exits. Mouse Three exits also.*]

NARRATOR:
> There are legends about singing
> —that our tribe once sang.
> And some of those songs
> survive but no one alive
> knows how to sing them.
> and we're sure of one thing
> —those are not the songs
> that Josephine sings. In fact,
> for some who listen to Josephine
> when she is with a group
> there is no distinction in her
> voice from the folk piping
> that everyone practices
> while they work or after
> dinner.
> We pipe like this:
> Peep—peep—peep—peep—
> peep—peep—peep—peep.
> Everybody does.

4

[*Mouse Three and Four pass through the spot of light together. Between them they carry a huge piece of Swiss cheese and two giant heads of wheat.*]

MOUSE THREE AND FOUR:
Peep—peep—peep—peep—
peep—peep—peep—peep.

[*Mouse Three and Four exit.*]

NARRATOR [*solo*]:
And we think nothing
of it. It's a soothing sound
to pipe. It's an automatic
sound—a tribal characteristic.

[*Mouse Two passes through the spot of light carrying a giant head of wheat.*]

MOUSE TWO:
Peep—peep—peep—peep.

[*He exits.*]

NARRATOR [*solo*]:
But no one ever thought
of it as Art. We hardly
note that we do it.

[*Mouse Three passes through the light.*]

MOUSE THREE:
Peep—peep—peep—peep.

[*He exits.*]

NARRATOR [*solo*]:
In fact, while we assemble
in huge crowds waiting with

5

warm but almost stoic anticipation
to hear Josephine we sometimes
listen to a child who has
forgotten to be silent and note
that the infant piping is not
so different from Josephine's
singing—except that the child
seems more adept
and
then
of
course
we wonder more about
ourselves and we stand there
in the driving rain—all of us
assembled—aware that the cat
is not too far away—and that
our never-ending and ceaseless
work is growing while we stand.
And we wait—and wait—in
anticipation of Josephine's
arrival while (I sometimes think)
she is watching from some secret place
to see if we have waited long enough
with solemn enough anticipation
to please her.

[*The Narrator rings his bell. The circle of light on him
goes black. The bell continues to ring quietly. There is a
faint regular drumbeat. A spot of light comes up on Josephine. She stands on a raised platform at the back center
of the stage. There is a large plaque on the raised platform.
It says "JOSEPHINE." She is in an ecstatic and intense posture with one arm raised. She is in a flowered white and
brown Victorian dress—as if she were a spotted mouse.
She has mouse ears and tail. She is delicate and beautiful
but gives a sense of great strength. Silver light pours from
her like an aura. She makes a brief tableau. Then she
leans her head and upper body—putting her hand up to*

shield her eyes—and stares intently into the place where the Narrator had been speaking. The drumbeat continues. The light fades on Josephine. There is the sound of the bell. The circle of light comes up again where the Narrator had been standing earlier. The rock and straw are gone.

[*The bell is now seen to be a bicycle bell. Sycophant One stands by the bicycle ringing the bell. She is dressed as per the other mice—tail, long mismatched dress, a broad-brimmed sunbonnet. Next to her is Sycophant Two. He has a big mustache and a workingman's jacket and cap.*]

SYCOPHANT ONE [*excited*]:
Josephine's going to appear
in her flowered dress!
How can she work and sing and be so beautiful
all at once?
The tribe should give her everything she wants.

SYCOPHANT TWO:
Yeah! Yes, you're right, Miss.

SYCOPHANT ONE:
Her little grace notes are perfection.
When she goes like this . . .

[*She imitates Josephine.*]

Peep—peep—peep—peep—
peep—peep—peep.

SYCOPHANT TWO [*interrupting*]:
Pardon me, Miss, don't imitate Josephine, Miss.
It's a travesty to do so. That's just folk-piping.

SYCOPHANT ONE:
Yes, you're right.
I told her how fine she is when her bosom heaves.
Like this . . .

7

[*She imitates Josephine's heaving bosom during singing.*]

   and like this—and . . . Oh! Ah!

SYCOPHANT TWO:
   Let's spread the word that she's feeling well
          despite all the work
          she's got to do.

SYCOPHANT ONE [*darting her eyes*]:
          You didn't hear the cat
              did you?

SYCOPHANT TWO:

              No.

SYCOPHANT ONE:
          Could it have been an owl?

SYCOPHANT TWO [*saluting One*]:
              No.

SYCOPHANT ONE [*hops on her bicycle*]:
          What ecstasy! She'll sing!

[*She rides the bike out of the light—ringing the bike bell as she goes. The light goes out.*]

[*Blackness. The bicycle bell is interspersed with a little clacking sound. The bike bell dies away. The clacking sound continues. A pool of light comes up on Mother Mouse, Father Mouse, and Baby. They are gathered around a fireplace with a little fire on the hearth. Mother is in a rocking chair knitting. Father leans on an imaginary mantel—bespectacled, smoking his pipe. Baby sits in front of the fire. Baby alternately pipes and clacks two little wooden dowels together. The sound is monorhythmic and not musical. Baby is a full-grown young man in short pants and a baby bonnet.*]

BABY:

Peep . . .

[*Clack of dowels*]

Peep . . .

[*Clack*]

Peep . . .

[*Clack*]

Peep . . .

[*Clack*]

Peep . . .

[*Clack*]

Peep . . .

[*Clack*]

FATHER MOUSE [*looking at a big watch on a chain*]:
Well!

[*He removes the baby bonnet from Baby and stands Baby up onto his feet. He takes the dowels away.*]

So, little one, childhood's at an end.

BABY:

Peep? Peep?

MOTHER:

Papa, is it over already?

FATHER [*to Baby*]:
Infancy can't last forever.
We're sorry.

BABY:

Peep?

9

MOTHER:
It's time to go to work, baby dear one.

BABY:

Peep?

MOTHER:

Yes. Labor calls.

BABY:

I like it here.

MOTHER:

You must join the tribe in work.
That's what Papa says.

BABY:

Do I Mama? Do I Papa?
Do I have to go out?

FATHER:

Yes.
We're a hard-working and serious
people—though we have our cunning.
There's no time
for childhood play
we
keep
—subsumed—
a sense
of humor.

MOTHER [*hands folded over her apron—looking at Baby*]:
That's right.

FATHER [*handing over a bag*]:
Here's your bag of tools.

BABY:

Thank you.

10

FATHER:
There's everything you'll need.

MOTHER [*opens imaginary door and shows Baby to it*]:
Have a good time in the world.

[*She kisses Baby.*]

FATHER [*shaking Baby's hand*]:
Stiff upper lip, son.
Watch out for the carnivores.

BABY [*walks stiffly through the imaginary door*]:
Thanks, Mom and Dad.

[*He closes the imaginary door behind him.*]

Peep . . . Peep . . . Peep . . . Peep . . .

[*He exits.*]

FATHER [*sighs*]:
Well.

MOTHER [*sighs*]:
Well.

FATHER:
That's that.
We grow up fast.

MOTHER:
I guess there's a lot . . .

FATHER:
A lot like him out there . . .

[*He gestures into the darkness.*]

11

MOTHER [*wiping a tear*]:
> Yes.

[*Pause. She changes the subject completely.*]

> That Josephine . . .

FATHER:
> The singer?

MOTHER:
> She wants exemption from work.

FATHER:
> Not labor?

MOTHER:
> That's right. She wants
> to sing more often
> and more beautifully.
> She says she will if she
> doesn't have to labor.

FATHER:
> Hmmm.

MOTHER:
> What do you think
> of that?

FATHER:
> Everybody works.
> That's crazy.

[*He taps the dowels together absentmindedly. The stage goes to blackness. The dowel taps turn into the ringing of a bicycle bell. The spot comes up, and Sycophant One rides through the light with her dress blowing in the wind.*]

12

SYCOPHANT ONE [*ecstatically imitating Josephine*]:
                    Peep. Peep. Peep.
                Josephine will sing soon!

[*Blackness. A pool of light comes up on the stage. The sound of the bicycle bell turns to light drumtaps. Josephine is intensely looking into an imaginary mirror. She has on an airy, sparkling, crownlike tiara. There are silk cloths draped over poles in a decorative way behind her.*

[*Josephine tears off the tiara and throws it on the floor and jumps up and down on it.*]

JOSEPHINE:
                    Darn it!

[*Prettily jumping up and down, crushing the tiara.*]

                Darn! Darn! Darn!

[*She looks around furiously.*]

        I'm so mad I could snap and bite!

[*She takes a little jump on the smashed tiara.*]

                    Darn!

[*She kicks the tiara out of the pool of light. She speaks contemptuously.*]

                    WHAT
                      I
                    WANT
                     IS
                  FREEDOM
                for my art!
              My songs are unique,
              immortal, different!

13

[*She poses beautifully in the posture of song.*]

Freedom for my art
and they could give it to me!
My songs serve the people.
My singing brings them
together
—even if they stand there
with noses in each other's fur,
or clothes, they know
when
they hear
my songs
that they're together.
That there's a transcendence
beyond everything and . . .

[*She jumps up and down lightly in a fury.*]

Oh damn! Darn!
They must learn to give me liberty
and freedom for what I want!
I'm reasonable!

[*She looks in her mirror.*]

I'll go to the court of judges.
They'll hear me!

[*She swirls a scarf over her shoulder. There is a background sound of occasional drumbeats.*]

I'll pull my reward like a rosy
freckled apple
from the highest
branch.

[*She coughs a little cough.*]

14

How weak I am.
I give my all
in singing.
I
burn
myself up
swiftly
—a bonfire of leaves
lit in many places.
I'm a hot red flame
with little smoke.
I'll
tell
them.

[*Josephine hurls on a light cape and begins to march vigorously, determinedly, and lightly. She walks in a spiraling pattern. The pool of light follows her around the bare stage.*]

I'll
let them know
once more!
I'm mad!
Oh darn!
I'll tell the judges to free me so I can sing.

[*Tableau of Josephine. Her arms upraised. Light pulls down to a tight spot on her and then goes out.*]

[*Blackness. A pool of light comes up on a crowd scene. Baby stands with his two wooden dowels and taps them as the drumbeats behind Josephine's speech fade. Baby's bag of tools is at his feet. He is full grown and vigorous. His baby pants have become lederhosen.*]

[*Various mice—including Mother Mouse and Father Mouse—stand about. They are all facing one direction. Many of them hold a pole with a crossbar on it. On the*] *crossbar is hung a coat or a dress, and there are mouse ears and tails—and wigs on the pole. The dressed poles are treated as members of the crowd. The real mice address the stick figures as if they are real. And they stand arm-in-arm with them. Though there may be only five or six real mice the effect is of a sizable crowd. They wait patiently.]*

BABY [*tapping sticks*]:
Peep.

[*Clack.*]
Peep.

[*Clack. Etc.*]

OTHER MICE:
Peep. Peep. Peep. Peep. Peep.

[*Etc.*]

SYCOPHANT ONE [*arrives on her bicycle, ringing the bike bell once or twice*]:
Wow! A good crowd!
Everyone's waiting
to hear her sing.
We're so lucky!

[*She pokes a mouse.*]

Hey!
We're lucky!
This will be
a concert!

MICE [*quietly, sometimes addressing one another, very self-contained*]:
Peep. Peep. Peep. [*Etc.*]

[*Pause. Quiet.*]

16

MOTHER MOUSE:
> Look, isn't that Baby?

FATHER MOUSE:
> Where?

MOTHER MOUSE:
> At the front of the crowd.

FATHER MOUSE:
> Hmm. Yeah.

BABY [*to Sycophant One*]:
> I love Josephine.
> I'll wait forever.

MOTHER MOUSE:
> He's grown up.
> Life is swift for us.

FATHER MOUSE:
> Hmm. Peep. Peep. [*Etc.*]

MICE:
> Peep. Peep. [*Etc.*]

[*Mice A, B, C, and D converse in the crowd.*]

MOUSE A:
> Do you think Josephine
> is worried 'cause
> she's getting older?
> Could
> she want
> special
> rewards
> and recognitions
> for that reason?

17

MOUSE B:

> She doesn't think
> that way.
> She's
> too
> self-centered.
> Probably thinks
> her songs are getting
> finer.

BABY [*a little angry*]:

> They are!
> They are getting finer, sweeter,
> richer.

MOUSE C:

> I agree.
> I was just talking.

MOUSE A:

> He's right. And, yes
> the songs are
> richer.

[*Slight pause*]

> I think.

MOUSE D:

> They sound like
> they always
> have.
> I can't tell any difference.

MOUSE E:

> Let's be quiet.

MOUSE A [*to Mouse D*]:

> You're here to listen
> aren't you?

18

MOUSE D:
> I wouldn't miss
> a concert.

[*Sycophant One rings her bike bell.*]

MOUSE E:
> SHH!

MICE [*quietly*]:
> Peep. Peep.

MOUSE D:
> Shhh.

[*Quiet*]

SYCOPHANT ONE [*ringing her bike bell*]:
> Josephine's coming.

BABY:
> Be quiet with the bell!
> There she is.

[*The light on the crowd dims to half-light. There are drum-beats as before. A spotlight comes up on Josephine. She is on a dais looking down at the crowd.*]

JOSEPHINE [*with hesitation but very firm*]:
> I . . .

[*Pause. She looks into the mouse crowd.*]

> I
> want to sing . . .

[*She looks into the crowd again.*]

> I
> want to sing
> my best for you.

19

I
want to sing
my best for you
though you do not
understand the meaning
or
the
beauty
of my songs.

[*She pauses, sweetly and reasonably, and with charm and daintiness.*]

I want all of you to feel the height
and nadir of what
my songs
can bring.
Each
of you can feel it.
Feel what I feel
from your paws nail
to your ear tips.
Everyone can know
the transcendence
that I feel
when I'm singing.
It
is
within
the reach
of all of you.

BABY:

We're listening!
We hear you!

[*The mice peep.*]

JOSEPHINE:

BUT
I
CAN
NOT
do my best.
I
sing for you
over and above
my daily labor.
After I sing
I must work
—you know I am delicate
and I cannot
recover my full
strength.
There is not time
to
rest.
Then there is some
great grief
or problem
and
I
must sing
and bring
you together
once again
and raise your
spirits
with
my songs.
It is a cycle.
I
sing
then I must
work.
Then I have

21

no rest
(for singing drains me)
but
then I
must sing
again—for you . . .
and I
am further
weakened.
Each
concert
comes
out of me
and is for you.
But
you
cannot
have the heights
of my potentialities.
YOU CANNOT HAVE THE WHOLE
SPIRIT
for
I
am constantly
weakened
in my great endeavor
for your benefit.
I am growing weaker
all the time.

[*She coughs*.]

I cough.

[*A sycophant mouse comes up an each side to lightly support her*.]

And I limp.
If you

22

will give
me my full
strength—as I
was meant to have
it for
my singing
—for my singing alone—
and grant me an exemption
from daily labor
—not because it is odious
to me—but
because my songs
and singing
are so much more
than labor
THEN,
THEN I
can sing
for you with
full devotion,
concentration, refined
skill primed with energy,
and highest art.
YOU
CAN
all
feel
what
I
feel.
You can be
like gods
of liberation.
But I am
chained
by
work.
—I grant you work is necessary
duty.

the moving of the moon
and the roaring
of the sea
and we know
KNOW
what you
ask
and it is our task,
Josephine, to tell you no!
The joy of work must never take a dimmer glow!
NO, JOSEPHINE!

[*Bangs gavel*]

NO!

[*Bangs gavel*]

NO!

[*Josephine swirls around in agony. She clutches her chest, tears her hair. There are swirling sounds from musical instruments, and the stage goes black.*]

JUDGE:

NO!

[*Bangs gavel*]

NO!

[*Bangs gavel*]

NO!

[*In the blackness is the blare of industrial factory buzzers, then a swirling sound of instruments or Moog synthesizer, then work buzzers again.*

26

[*A spot of light comes up on Josephine. She is in front of an imaginary mirror. There are poles with silk hangings on them behind her.*

[*In the pool of light with Josephine are Sycophant One and Sycophant Two. A faint drumbeat replaces the industrial work buzzer, then the drumbeat diminishes.*]

JOSEPHINE [*bending her tiara back into shape and trying it in front of a mirror*]:
                    Therefore . . .

[*Pause. She looks in the mirror.*]

                    Therefore,
                         I,
                    can . . .
                    Hmmm.

[*She adjusts her tiara. Pause*]

                I can only know
            the fullest extent of my songs
                if I am allowed to sing
                    them fully and with
                all my love and strength
                and vigor. The subtleties
            and the great extent the songs
                    may reach is
                    like a mystery
                    of blackness
                    extending
                ten trillion miles . . .

[*Pause*]

                extending ten trillion
                miles into one solid
            mystery like the sculpture

27

SYCOPHANT ONE:

>That's right.

JOSEPHINE:

>Be quiet!

[*She walks in the light as it moves.*]

>There's
>no
>way out
>for me unless
>in some way I
>can pluck down
>the garland
>and place it on
>my head.
>AH,
>but
>it is more than
>that—the garland
>has no worth unless
>its value is freedom.

SYCOPHANT TWO:

>Everyone stands
>in your concerts
>in total silence
>and they listen
>as best they can . . .

SYCOPHANT ONE:

>Everyone comes
>to hear you.

JOSEPHINE:

>It's not enough!
>They
>do
>not

30

hear!
They only hear the limits
of their ears
reflecting
the limitations
that they place
on me.
They're
deaf
and
dumb
and I wish
to make them free.
I can take them with me
to the farthest edges
that I see.

SYCOPHANT TWO:

They're full of reverence.

JOSEPHINE:

It's dull.

SYCOPHANT ONE:

They honor you.

JOSEPHINE:

It's honor from the stupid.

SYCOPHANT TWO:

And . . .

JOSEPHINE:

But I can make them bright!
The songs of possibility that I feel
can turn them into stars.

SYCOPHANT ONE:

They say there's never
been another like you.

NO!

[*There are swirling sounds from the musical instruments or Moog. The Judge leans maniacally forward to the Josephine tableau.*]

NO!

[*Bangs gavel*]

NO!

[*Bangs gavel*]

NO!

[*Sycophant One looks around wildly and idiotically rings her bike bell. The light goes off on the judges. There is a swirling sound of musical instruments. Josephine is caught in the swirl, and she spins around—falls—and cries out in a scream. Sycophant Two bends over Josephine confusedly.*]

SYCOPHANT TWO [*to Sycophant One*]:
Look, look, Miss.
She's fallen in a faint.

SYCOPHANT ONE:
Yeah! Oooh! Ooh! It's
scary! Did you hear
a cat?

JOSEPHINE [*getting up*]:
OH! Oh! Oh!

[*Enraged with sycophants*]

I'm going to
get you!
I
hate

34

you
all! I
can't stand
your ass kissing.
Everyone
is
like
all
the others.
Oh pig meat!

[*She bites Sycophant Two.*]

There!

SYCOPHANT TWO:

Help! Help!
Don't, Miss!
You bit me,
Miss!

JOSEPHINE [*cursing*]:
Pig meat! Dog pearls!

[*She bites him again and claws out scratching simultaneously at Sycophant One. Sycophant Two shouts in terror and runs off. Josephine hurls herself around in swirling patterns and cries out: "Peep! Peep! Musk! Duck feet!" Sycophant One stands in fascinated horror and rings her bike bell desultorily. There is a drumbeat. Josephine grabs Sycophant One.*]

JOSEPHINE:

Bite!

[*Bites her*]

Bite!

[*Sycophant One runs off.*]

35

like
her type)—
she could outwork
any of
us.

TOP HAT [*picking his teeth*]:
Quite a worker.

SPATS:

She's never slacked off
ever.
But
no
one
in our tribe
ever does.

TOP HAT:

That's right.

HEADBAND [*gesturing*]:
Yo!
Get 'em off!

[*Apples have been traded for wheat and vice versa. The trolleys are hauled off in opposite directions into the darkness.*

[*Josephine is left solo in the light. She climbs up exhaustedly and daintily on a little box that was left behind when the trolleys left.*]

JOSEPHINE:

I'll practice.

[*She throws back her shoulders, spreads her arms. She becomes momentarily inspired. She begins to sing.*]

38

Peep . . . Peep . . .
Peep . . .

[*She is dejected.*]

No!
That's
not
it.

[*She limps.*]

[*Two girl mice enter.*]

GIRL MOUSE ONE:
Let us help you!

GIRL MOUSE TWO:
You're limping. Here!

[*Josephine pulls back.*]

JOSEPHINE:
I'm in a perfect rapture.
I'm
ecstatically
contemplating
song.
I
don't
need you!

[*She pushes them.*]

Get away.
You'll
put
me

39

JOSEPHINE:

Sure, yes, and sable silhouettes
of our joys built cities
and opened shops and performed
operas on the cliff tops
among the endless
forests of our feelings.
Satin eagles in clown
masks took us from
our bed of petals
and flew us
to
the
sunset.
I
remember
all
of
that!
Now
stop!
STOP!
I'm walking away.
I do not know
you.
That was
a
moment!
It is all past.
Now is now.
Those vistas were
stage sets for the comedy
of imagination.
I'm
in search of . . .

BABY:

You're after me.

42

JOSEPHINE:

. . . in search of the real,
the reality of song.

BABY:

My arms are songs.

JOSEPHINE:

My songs are arms.

BABY:

My body tells me
you must have my babies.

JOSEPHINE:

Disgusting! We'd be
like any others! Growing
paunchy! Turning stupid.
Freed of aspirations we'd be
dull bags of flesh.
We'd
be
as
all
the others.
There'd be
no difference.

BABY:

I love you!

JOSEPHINE:

Can you hear me?
You love me because I am
different—I am Josephine
the Singer. But the feelings
—all the fireworks—fly
between

43

[*Drumbeats turn to ringing of the bike bell.*

[*The light comes up on a group of mice—Sycophants One and Two and others. They are seated at a table.*]

SYCOPHANT ONE [*ringing the bike bell*]:
Meeting called to order.

SYCOPHANT TWO AND OTHERS:
Hear! Hear!

FIRST MOUSE:
We must relieve Josephine
and obtain, for her, an exemption
from
odious
labor.

SECOND MOUSE:
All right.

THIRD MOUSE:
What can we do?

SYCOPHANT TWO:
Why don't we do this orderly, sirs?
We've been called to order.

SYCOPHANT ONE:
That's right.
I called us to order.

FIRST MOUSE:
It's now or never.
We must do something.

THIRD MOUSE:
I agree.

46

SECOND MOUSE:

We've been called to order.

SYCOPHANT ONE [*ringing bell*]:

We'll begin.
George, what do you say?

SYCOPHANT TWO:

I think first we should get
ourselves level. Take off
our caps and scratch our heads.

[*He scratches his head.*]

FIRST MOUSE:

I second that!

SECOND MOUSE:

Shall we vote?

SYCOPHANT ONE:

Shhhhhh!

THIRD MOUSE:

I have an idea.

ALL:

Hear!

THIRD MOUSE:

We could
go to bed and sleep
till
Josephine
receives the exemption
that she's
after.

new passions
to
do
it!

SYCOPHANT TWO:

Nothing like it
has ever been done before.
It's unthinkable.

THIRD MOUSE:

Well, tell it.

SYCOPHANT TWO [*warming to it*]:
Oh, it's a scary one.

SYCOPHANT ONE:

Nothing is as scary as a cat.

NEW MOUSE:

That gave me a chill.
Don't say that.

THIRD MOUSE [*to Sycophant Two*]:
Tell us.

SYCOPHANT TWO:

Well, here it is, sirs and ma'ams,
we set up our own court.

NEW MOUSE [*shocked*]:

No!

BABY [*to himself*]:

Maybe this is it!

SYCOPHANT TWO:

And some of us are judges . . .

FIRST MOUSE:

Bravo!

SYCOPHANT ONE:

And since we're the only judges
we give Josephine what
she wants.

FIRST MOUSE:

We'll do it!

SECOND MOUSE:

An ad hoc court!

SEVERAL MICE:

Hooray!

SYCOPHANT TWO:

Now, there's one trick to it.
One flaw.

FIRST MOUSE:

What?

SYCOPHANT TWO:

Why will the people pay
any attention to us
when they're used
to the other
court of judges?

BABY [*to himself*]:

Yes?

SECOND MOUSE:

Yes. Why?

SYCOPHANT TWO:

I've thought about it . . .

51

SECOND MOUSE:

Me too.
See you later.

SYCOPHANT ONE:

Meeting adjourned.
Try to think of something.

[*The mice walk out of the light one at a time.*]

SYCOPHANT TWO [*stands saying good night to an exiting mouse*]:

'Night, Miss!

SYCOPHANT ONE:

George, we've got to be realistic.

SYCOPHANT TWO [*humbly*]:

Yes.
No more crazy ideas—ever.

SYCOPHANT ONE:

It's got to be peaceable.

SYCOPHANT TWO:

Yes.

[*Sycophant One rides her bike out of the light. She rings the bell. Sycophant Two leaves. The light goes black on Baby. The stage is black. There is a drumbeat. A spot of light comes up on Josephine. She is adjusting her hair in front of an imaginary mirror. There are silk cloths draped over poles behind her. She poses in front of the mirror as if she were singing. There are drumbeats timed with her exclamations.*]

JOSEPHINE:

Ah!

54

[*She peers into a mirror.*]

Oh!

[*Peers*]

Mmmm!

[*Peers*]

[*Baby crawls into the spot of light. He is behind Josephine. She does not see him as he enters.*]

BABY:
Josephine.

[*The clack of dowels is heard in the blackness.*]

I'm here.

[*Clack of dowels in the blackness*]

You cannot hide
from me.
I'll find you
anywhere.

JOSEPHINE [*she tries to push Baby out*]:
I hate you!

[*She hurls her tiara against the floor, and it bounces out of the light.*]

BABY:
Josephine, all I can
think of is the kingdom
of our love. Be my
queen!

55

JOSEPHINE [*furious*]:
Yes! That's it! You
want a queen and not
a singer.
A
QUEEN
is nothing.
The
SINGER
is the highest
gift
to our tribe.
Like all the rest
—like any enemy—
you
foul
my gifts.
You do not care for my singing.
You want me to press
out babies
from between my thighs
like any female
of
our people.
You
are just another
meaty twirl
in dark softness
and
you
see
me
in your
image!

BABY [*writhing on the floor*]:
Josephine, I'll make
you whole. Complete.
Oh,

56

please, please,
love me!

JOSEPHINE:

Yes, you are
worse
than my enemies
—who only hate my singing
and attempt to end my songs!
You would end me by
turning me into a sack
of flesh to satisfy your pleasure.

BABY:

The pleasure
is our love.
The flesh overcomes
itself and turns
into spirit . . .

JOSEPHINE:

And the highest spirit
is in the swirling
of the greatest voice
in
air.

BABY:

I'll kill myself.

JOSEPHINE [*furious*]:

Do it!
Kill
your
self!

BABY:

I said I'd end myself
for you!
You don't want me to die!

57

JOSEPHINE:

DO IT!

BABY:

You want me to?

JOSEPHINE [*jumping up and down in fury*]:
Kill yourself!
Yes!
Do
it
now!

BABY:

Me? Your lover?

JOSEPHINE:

Hurry! Hurry!
I
hate
you!
You
be-
little
me.
You see me as a sack of sex and not a singer!

[*She jumps up and down.*]

Do it!
Do it!

BABY [*horrified*]:

NO!

JOSEPHINE:

Yes, do it now.

[*She turns on her heel and walks angrily out of the light.*

58

Baby takes out a knife and looks at it and looks up at the audience.

[*Light goes out on Baby.*

[*Blackness*

[*The Narrator's bell is ringing in the blackness.*

[*A spotlight comes up. The spotlight is empty except for a large rock and oversized straw around it. The bell continues ringing.*

[*Mouse One—from scene one, with the handlebar mustache —walks through the light. Mouse One is carrying a giant ear of wheat. He peeps as he passes through the light.*

[*Mouse Two—from scene one, with the bowler hat, wig, and cigar—walks into the light peeping and carrying a giant apple. He sets the apple down to rest and peeps to himself.*

[*The Narrator's bell continues from the blackness.*

[*Mouse Two picks up the giant apple and hurries out of the light.*

[*The Narrator steps into the light. He is ringing his bell.*]

NARRATOR [*to Mouse Two, who has exited*]:
> Hey! Hey! Wait a min!

MOUSE TWO [*steps back into the light and waves*]:
> Must rush, old chop!

[*Exits*]

NARRATOR [*steps up on the rock*]:
> There. Ah.

Let's see. I'll tell
it to myself again.
I'll just think out loud and push
this through in that way. Ah,
let me see . . .

[*Thoughtfully*]

The skull is like
a spark
for it glimmers with what
is going on: information
sent
to
it
by the flesh
and everything
around us. Josephine
feels as if she is not a spark
but a roaring bonfire of leaves
that lights the late summer sky
and we
are snails
that come in crowds
to watch the flames.

[*He turns around on the rock trying to get comfortable.*]

—And I guess we are.

[*Thoughtfully*]

But then also . . .

[*Mouse Three with a long white beard enters.*]

Hey, wait a moment!

MOUSE THREE:
All right, brother.

NARRATOR [*ringing his bell*]:
I'm talking about Josephine.

MOUSE THREE:
Of course you are.

NARRATOR:
She brings us together.

MOUSE THREE:
That's right.

NARRATOR:
And she says we're ungrateful.
It's real transcendent beauty
she brings us—she claims.

MOUSE THREE [*trying to get away*]:
Listen, I've got to go . . .

NARRATOR:
Wait.
Even those who feel her singing is nothing
but a kind of folk-piping put on the stage
for us to see ourselves do not deny
that she is special—more sensitive,
brilliant—maybe thrilling . . .

MOUSE THREE:
Everyone knows there's never been
another one like her.
See you!

[*Exits*]

NARRATOR [*looks at his bell, rings it, speaks to it*]:
So we are like the kindly father
who—even insulted by a daughter—
realizes the insult is a hand stretched

61

out for aid—imploring—and we take
the hand and lead the child—or give
support. But like a kindly
and just father, the tribe will go
only so far—and no farther.
What
may
be
strange
and what Josephine
can see so plainly—and what
others do not see—is the contradiction
in our nature and in our treatment
of Josephine. Because our lives
are like such meteors, flaming briefly,
brightly, we have little childhood. There's
little time for play or games before the nec-
essaries draw us out into the world. Therefore,
always, there's a sad sweetness, a tender generosity
toward what is childlike, yet . . .
Yet,
little
as it matters
in the main, the judges—
who only speak the voices of the people—
say *no* very harshly to Josephine's plea.
We
know
that in fact
if we granted
what she wants
she'd go ahead and work
anyway . . .

[*He looks into the darkness and speaks to someone there.*]

Isn't that right?

[*A mouse steps into the light.*]

MOUSE:
Why, yes, I think so.

NARRATOR:
Do you think what she is doing
is singing—or is it some emotional
exhibition?

MOUSE:
I know I like it.

NARRATOR:
Do you think she holds
the people together and props
us up with her voice in times
of trouble and famine?

MOUSE:
I'm not one for heavy thinking.

NARRATOR:
Do you think she
should be free of labor?

MOUSE:
Of course not.
I've got to go now!

[*Exits*]

NARRATOR [*solo again*]:
And strangest of all—and how it ties in
with the people's feelings for Josephine
probably no one can fathom—is
that when we assemble in huge crowds
to listen to Josephine, we do so at
a lot of risk
to our
lives.

63

The messengers go out
to bring us the news that she's
chosen to sing—and we hurry
to the spot and stand there expectantly
and silently till there's enough
of us to cause her
to begin her singing.
And just as she often sings in
times of greatest danger to the people,
she often chooses—stock still
in her tracks and inspired by the song
in her—to sing in the most
dangerous places.
There are places most dangerous
to our tribe—spots where the cat
may creep up on us unobserved,
or where the owl may silently
and suddenly swoop
from a corner of darkness,
where even
the cleverest sentries cannot
spot him.
Those places
are
often
chosen by Josephine
and we assemble there as willingly
as any other. The result is that often
many deaths terminate
the concert. The ground
is covered with the bodies
of our people—but Josephine
is
the
first
to
flee.
Indeed
she's whisked

away at once by
her entourage.
AND
it is probably
the sound of her singing
—wavery and weak as it seems to some—
that attracted the enemy.
These
things
seem strange to me.
As much as I admire
her, I'm glad to see a concert
end with her notes and not with
cries of death and terror.
I'm always relieved when we
walk silently away at concert's
end and gradually begin our
folk-piping.

[*Light comes up on Josephine, who is on a dais. She is finishing a song. She is in an ecstatic posture. It is a drawnout piping.*]

JOSEPHINE:
Peeee-e-e-e-e-e-ep . . .

[*The light dims out on Josephine. The Narrator rings his bell. The light comes up on a little crowd of mice. They are silent for a moment as the bell rings.*]

MOUSE:
I guess that was the end
of the concert?

MOUSE:
Shhhh.

MOUSE [*whispering*]:
Yes. I think so.

65

MOUSE:

                Shall we leave now?

MOUSE:

                I feel fulfilled.

MOUSE:

                I'm relieved there
                was no cat this time.

MOUSE:

                Remember
                two
                concerts
                ago?

MOUSE:

                It was awful.

MOUSE:

                So many killed
                and wounded.

MOUSE:

                That ugly field
                with the boulders
                scares me.
                I
                knew
                when Josephine
                chose that place to sing
                there'd be trouble.

MOUSE:

                How many died?

MOUSE:

                A lot!

MOUSE:

Shhhhhhhh.

MOUSE:

We should be
quiet for a while
after a concert.

MOUSE:

Yeah.

MOUSE:

Yes.

[*The crowd exits into the darkness as the Narrator—in another spotlight—rings his bell. Both spotlights fade. There is the sound of little "jester" bells that are sewed to the clothing of mouse ghosts.*

[*A spotlight comes up on a field of large stones.*

[*Lying in the field of stones are three mouse ghosts. Their faces are spotted with gore and red ribbons flutter on them. There are little bells on the ribbons. The mouse ghosts lie in terrible postures of death. It is a tableau of the aftermath of a scene of carnage. There are large pools of blood.*]

MOUSE GHOST ONE [*opening his eyes, sitting up a little, looking at himself*]:
We been dead a while.

MOUSE GHOST TWO [*waking*]:
Yeah. That's right.

MOUSE GHOST THREE [*a girl mouse, waking*]:
Hi!
We dead?

67

MOUSE GHOST TWO:
                    Yeah. That's right.

MOUSE GHOST ONE:
                    Shall we do the dance
                    of death?

MOUSE GHOST TWO:
                         That's about
                         all we can do.

MOUSE GHOST THREE:
                         O.K.

[*The mouse ghosts stand up and do a beautiful, angular, awkward dance. They are accompanied by their bells and the sound of dowels clacking. When one mouse ghost speaks he stops. The others stop motionless and frozen in position while he speaks.*]

MOUSE GHOST ONE:
                    Do you blame Josephine?
                    For getting us killed and everything?

[*The mouse ghosts dance a step or two.*]

MOUSE GHOST TWO:
                    No. That's just the way
                         things go.

[*They dance a step or two.*]

MOUSE GHOST THREE:
                         It's O.K.

[*They dance a step or two.*]

MOUSE GHOST TWO:
                         Yeah.

68

[*They dance.*]

MOUSE GHOST TWO:
We never laugh when Josephine
sings.

[*They dance.*]

MOUSE GHOST ONE:
And we certainly
love laughter
even for its own sake.

[*They dance.*]

MOUSE GHOST THREE:
And there's something
laughable about Josephine
and the way she postures.

[*They dance.*]

MOUSE GHOST TWO:
I was one of those who said
her singing is nothing
out of the ordinary
but
is only
a kind
of folk-piping . . .

[*They dance.*]

MOUSE GHOST THREE:
That's right.

[*They dance.*]

MOUSE GHOST TWO:
But when Josephine sang I'd

69

                  stand there as transported
                       by the song
                          as any
                     adolescent.

[*They dance a step.*]

MOUSE GHOST ONE [*stops, points into the darkness*]:
              Look at that guy coming toward
              us in the blackness.

[*They dance a step or two.*]

MOUSE GHOST TWO [*peering out of the light*]:
                  Yeah. Look at that!

[*They dance.*]

MOUSE GHOST TWO:
                     I love this dancing.

[*Sadly*]

                  Even if it is all we can do.

[*They dance.*]

MOUSE GHOST ONE [*points into the blackness*]:
                You know who that is?

MOUSE GHOST TWO:
                        Who?

MOUSE GHOST THREE:
                     Yeah, who?

MOUSE GHOST ONE:
                   That's Baby.

[*They dance a step or two.*]

MOUSE GHOST TWO:
Baby, the son of Mother and Father?

[*They dance a step or two.*]

MOUSE GHOST ONE:
That's right.
That's Baby.

MOUSE GHOST TWO:
Why's he crawling?

MOUSE GHOST THREE:
Dummy!

MOUSE GHOST ONE:
Because he's dead.

MOUSE GHOST TWO:
Oh.

[*They dance.*]

MOUSE GHOST ONE:
He grew up so fast . . .

MOUSE GHOST THREE:
Like all of us.

MOUSE GHOST ONE:
. . . that before he knew it
he was full grown.
And he fell
in love
with Josephine.

71

MOUSE GHOST TWO:
Oh no!

[*The mouse ghosts dance, and Baby crawls into the light. He has red ribbons on him also. His hands are all bloody.*]

BABY [*to the mouse ghosts*]:
Hey! Hey!

[*The mouse ghosts dance a few more steps, then they stop by Baby.*]

MOUSE GHOST ONE:
Hi, Baby.

MOUSE GHOST TWO:
Hi.

MOUSE GHOST THREE:
Hello.

[*The mouse ghosts dance.*]

BABY:
I killed myself.

[*He shows them a bloody knife.*]

MOUSE GHOST ONE [*stops*]:
Yes. I can see.

[*The mouse ghosts dance.*]

BABY:
Wait!

[*The mouse ghosts stop.*]

72

MOUSE GHOST TWO:

        Sure.

BABY:

        I killed myself for Josephine.

MOUSE GHOST TWO:

        You could say we did too.

BABY:

        But this is different.

MOUSE GHOST THREE:

        How?

BABY:

        She debased me.

MOUSE GHOST ONE:

        Let's dance.

BABY:

        Sure.

[*The mouse ghosts and Baby begin to dance in a ring. They stop.*]

BABY:

        All I wanted was for her
        to go on loving me.

MOUSE GHOST ONE:

        What do you mean?

BABY:

        I know she loved me.
        Our love was perfect
        and beautiful

73

full
of
fire
and warm nests of feathers
and smells of baking bread
and lighted cities walked about
by lions.
But
she
hated me
because I
loved her body.

MOUSE GHOST TWO:
That's strange.

[*They dance.*]

BABY:
I know the body is spirit.
But she said only her songs
are the highest
shape of things.

[*They dance.*]

BABY:
She said that even her enemies
don't try to colonize
her by making
babies.

[*They dance.*]

MOUSE GHOST THREE:
I don't know.

[*They dance.*]

BABY:

> I said our love was the purest
> thing. But she
> told me
> to kill
> myself.

MOUSE GHOST TWO:

> Did she
> really
> want that?

BABY:

> I guess so.

[*They dance.*]

[*Josephine appears in a spotlight walking toward the
three ghost mice and Baby as they dance. Josephine is
accompanied by a faint irregular drumbeat.*]

JOSEPHINE [*to herself*]:

> . . . And so pure beauty
> must be formed
> into song and I
> must keep myself
> open
> to
> the
> action . . .
> In fact,
> I must not
> question
> the processes . . .

[*Pause*]

> It is that simple.

75

[*The ghost mice and Baby are all invisible to, and unheard by, Josephine.*]

GHOST MOUSE ONE [*rattling bells*]:
          Hey, Josephine!

JOSEPHINE [*meditatively*]:
          I must not question
          the processes.
          It is that
          simple
          and . . .

BABY:
          Look, I'm dead!

[*There is a riffle of drumbeats and bells as Josephine enters the light wherein ghost mice and Baby are moving.*]

BABY [*grasping Josephine*]:
          Look at the knife, Josephine!
          See the blood on it.
          The blood
          is
          ME!
          Look, I did it!

JOSEPHINE [*removing Baby's hand unconsciously and without seeing him*]:
          Every
          day
          I must think this
          through,
          and a million times
          an instant
          I must feel it fresh.

GHOST MOUSE TWO [*madly dancing in front of Josephine*]:
          Hey, Josephine!

GHOST MOUSE ONE [*waving his hands in front of Josephine's face*]:

Josephine!

JOSEPHINE:

I must feel it fresh
a million times
an instant.
I
keep
the ordered
disorder
and the harmonious
disharmony.

BABY:

It's me! Me! Baby!
Look, I did it.
You wanted me to and I
did it.

[*Josephine thrusts Baby aside.*]

JOSEPHINE:

And it is all perfect.
It is an unceasing
effort
and
at the same
time it is my
nature
to keep that balance
and though it strains me
like the ultimate effort
it is also no
effort
at
all.
But

it is not
effortless.

[*The mouse ghosts and Baby are dancing all around Jo-sephine.*]

MOUSE GHOST THREE:
Woooo! Woooo!
We're haunting you!

JOSEPHINE:

I seek perfection
of song but it is
unavoidable. It will
be. The rose
makes effort
to create petals
and
yet there
WILL
BE
petals . . .
Without petals
there is no rose.
So
there
is both
perfection
and effort
—and there is none.

BABY:

Look, at the real
blood that poured
from my
chest.
You
can-
not

78

be heartless.
I know you can
see us.

[*Josephine pushes the mouse ghosts and Baby away without seeing them.*]

JOSEPHINE:

So,
there
is both
perfection
and effort
—and there is none.
Exactly
as matter
comes into
being from other
spaces—thrust there
by unmeasurable
effort
—and yet when it
is here
and present
it is so stable
and so calm,
like a *perfect*
visionary
song.

[*Josephine walks away. The light follows her and dims. Drumbeats disappear.*]

JOSEPHINE [*departing*]:

Yes,
that is it.
Songs are like
matter thrust here
from

other
dimensions
with
great
effort
but
yet
—in
their arrival—
are
all so stable
and so calm.
Songs, like life,
are the ultimate
contradiction.

[*Black on Josephine.*]

BABY [*sits down on the rock, head in hands*]:
I'm depressed.

MOUSE GHOST TWO:
Don't feel bad.
It happens to everybody.

MOUSE GHOST THREE:
Yeah. Sooner or later.

MOUSE GHOST ONE:
We're just dead. That's all.

MOUSE GHOST TWO:
Yeah.

MOUSE GHOST THREE:
This is O.K.
This is the way
it's supposed
to be.

MOUSE GHOST ONE:
We're supposed to be dead.
Or we wouldn't be dead.

MOUSE GHOST THREE:
Yeah, I agree.

BABY:
That's all right for you
because you died accidentally.

MOUSE GHOST ONE:
Everything's accident.

MOUSE GHOST TWO:
Maybe nothing is.

MOUSE GHOST ONE:
One thing is sure.

MOUSE GHOST THREE:
What?

MOUSE GHOST ONE:
We're dead.
So let's *be* dead.

BABY:
I don't want to be.

MOUSE GHOST ONE:
Well, you are.
Lie back down and face
the facts.

MOUSE GHOST TWO [*lying down*]:
Bye!

81

MOUSE GHOST THREE [*lying down*]:
>
> Night!

BABY [*trying to get up*]:
>
> I want to leave!

MOUSE GHOST ONE [*restraining Baby*]:
>
> You can't.
> This is it. We're
> dead.

BABY:
>
> I never wanted this.

MOUSE GHOST ONE:
>
> Be quiet.

[*They all lie down among the rocks. They assume postures of death and close their eyes.*]

[*A procession of mice enters the light. As they enter they clack dowels together nonrhythmically. There is a mouse in a stocking cap and a mouse in a purple dress and other mice.*]

STOCKING CAP [*looking around*]:
>
> There are a lot of them dead all right.

PURPLE DRESS [*shuddering*]:
>
> The field of rocks is very scary.

STOCKING CAP [*pointing to Baby*]:
>
> Look at that one.

ANOTHER MOUSE:
>
> Looks like the suicide.

PURPLE DRESS:
>
> That's him.

82

ANOTHER MOUSE:

> I'm frightened.

STOCKING CAP [*pointing to Mouse Ghost One*]:

> I used to move apples
> with him.

PURPLE DRESS [*pointing to Mouse Ghost Three*]:

> She and I grew
> up together. She was
> as cute as a button.
> Oooooh,
> look at the blood.

ANOTHER MOUSE:

> It could have been
> you or me just
> as easy.

PURPLE DRESS:

> We ought to all tell
> Josephine
> how we feel.

STOCKING CAP:

> Part of the reason we can't
> is that *she* says so little . . .

ANOTHER MOUSE:

> She's laconic.

ANOTHER MOUSE:

> No, it's something else.

PURPLE DRESS [*venturing*]:

> Cold . . .

STOCKING CAP:

> No, it's more than that . . .

PURPLE DRESS:
I adore her singing as much
as any but I can't talk
to her. After a concert she walks
away with eyes that
are flashing
but they don't move when
they flash.
I
don't
think
she cares
about who is
dead or dying.

[*The mice walk in the spotlight away from the bodies.*]

ANOTHER MOUSE:
She says her songs
have nothing to do
with that
but
are composed of the essences
of things and thoughts.

[*The bike bell is heard ringing. While the spotlight re-
mains on the conversing mice another spotlight comes up
on Josephine. She is limping and supported by an aide.
Sycophant One pushes her bike along ringing the bell.
There is a faint drumbeat.*]

SYCOPHANT ONE:
Make way for Josephine!

[*She rings her bell.*]

Josephine is coming.

84

JOSEPHINE:

I've strained my leg in laboring!
My
songs
will suffer
from this—and the tribe
will be the ultimate losers.
Singing
that is more beautiful
than love should not
be lost
by a people
who are in need of music.

PURPLE DRESS [*in the other spotlight with Stocking Cap,
etc.*]:

What she does not know
—some of the old mice say—
is that if it were
truly singing
or real music
of great breadth
then we would not listen
or we would
be alarmed.
In fact,
they say
it is only
a token, the merest
shadow
of music,
that we will allow
ourselves to listen to . . .

STOCKING CAP:

I don't understand.

ANOTHER MOUSE:

That's cynical.

85

SYCOPHANT ONE [*in the other spotlight and speaking to Josephine*]:

> Could you be asking
> too much
> of the
> judges?

JOSEPHINE:

> It is like a vulgar trick.
> The tribe gives me all
> I want
> —I mean
> they fancy
> that they give
> me what I want
> by giving me their
> dull attentions.
> *Then*
> they
> hold
> back
> and keep from me
> the prime necessity
> that would make my songs
> completely blossom.
> It
> is
> liberty
> for
> *ART*
> that I demand.
> I know my enemies claim it is revolution.
> Nothing like what I ask has ever
> happened so it is seen
> as
> a
> threat.

SYCOPHANT ONE:

> It is a crown on the highest branch.

86

JOSEPHINE:
> I'd rather have it higher than lower.
> Stop here. I'm going to think.

PURPLE DRESS [*in another spotlight*]:
> We must tell Josephine about
> the dead we've seen and all
> the dying that goes on.

STOCKING CAP:
> Do you think she cares?

PURPLE DRESS:
> Well,
> yes,
> I think she would.
> She does not think of the deaths
> as related to her concerts.
> She sees those deaths,
> like
> songs,
> as acts of Nature.

ANOTHER MOUSE:
> Let's tell her.

PURPLE DRESS:
> O.K.
> We'll practice
> telling her.

PURPLE DRESS [*calling into the darkness*]:
> Josephine.

STOCKING CAP:
> *Josephine!*

ANOTHER MOUSE [*calling out*]:
> Josephine,

there's too much death
and dying.

PURPLE DRESS [*calling to Josephine*]:
You must be reasonable!

STOCKING CAP:
That's how we'll
tell her.

PURPLE DRESS:
Remember when she was once
told that her songs were
folk-piping modified
to be singing
by the subtlety
of her consciousness?

ANOTHER MOUSE:
I'll never forget it.
Josephine gave me a chill.

PURPLE DRESS:
No mouse ever made
a face like that
before!

ANOTHER MOUSE:
It made my skin crawl.

PURPLE DRESS:
It was a smile of such
arrogance and haughty
contempt
that it tattooed itself
on my memory
forever.
Even from the back rows
I could see it.

STOCKING CAP:
> It's about time to go back to work.

[*They begin walking off. The spotlight moves with them.*]

ANOTHER MOUSE:
> Wait for me.

[*Black on Purple Dress, Stocking Cap, etc. Drumbeats. Josephine stands up in her pool of light and leans on an aide. She pushes the aide away.*]

JOSEPHINE:
> Get away from me!
> Get out of my sight. I've got
> to think. I must
> fill
> with inspiration.

SYCOPHANTS:
> Yes. Yes, Josephine.

JOSEPHINE:
> Rainbows are melting on gossamer
> and turning into vocal music.

[*The sycophants leave.*]

> The multiple existence of everything
> is thrusting itself
> outward through
> me.
> I am the extension and the welding
> together of every realm of real
> and unreal
> making every gesture in every shape.

[*Two mouse lovers enter Josephine's pool of light.*]

LOVER ONE [*pause*]:
 We're here, darling. You must choose
 between us for your true love.

LOVER TWO:
 We are your worshipers!

JOSEPHINE:
 How awful!
 Do you want my body
 or my songs?

LOVER TWO:
 We want your songs . . .

JOSEPHINE:
 At last!

LOVER ONE:
 We want your songs . . .

LOVER TWO [*continuing*]:
 For we know your
 songs are your physicality
 melted
 into
 air
 in vocal patterns.

JOSEPHINE:
 Then you want what
 you can touch?

LOVER ONE:
 If we can touch your songs
 then we want them.

JOSEPHINE:
 I see you're

after me!
You are worse than
the last lover. At
least he's gone now.
He's gone
somewhere.

LOVER TWO:

He killed himself.

LOVER ONE:

Just as you told him.

LOVER TWO:

He's dead.

LOVER ONE:

And we'll kill ourselves
unless you surrender
your love to us.

JOSEPHINE:
What do you mean "killed himself"?

LOVER ONE:

With a knife.

LOVER TWO:

He dances with the ghosts.

LOVER ONE:

Take me for your lover.

LOVER TWO:

Take me!

LOVER ONE:

Or I will kill myself.

LOVER TWO:

And I too!

LOVER ONE:

Each lost lover—says our people—
turns into two.

LOVER TWO:

Love is a Hydra
—each severed head is replaced in double.

JOSEPHINE:

Baby can't be dead!

LOVER ONE:

Some being like him has been
born a hundred times
since he died. We're a fertile people . . .

LOVER TWO:

And you need love.
You
are
not some cold
moon thing.

LOVER ONE:

We have knives and we
will kill ourselves as
he did
unless
you take
our love.

[*Lovers One and Two get on their knees in front of Josephine.*]

JOSEPHINE:

Oh, where is Baby? Baby is dead!

92

[*Josephine rushes out of the light.*]

LOVER ONE [*calling after Josephine*]:
    He's where one goes all too easily.

LOVER TWO [*calling to Josephine*]:
    Love us or we'll kill ourselves!

LOVER ONE [*to Lover Two, holding up a knife*]:
    Shall we do it now?

LOVER TWO [*looking at his knife*]:
    Let's give her one more chance.

LOVER ONE:

    We may have to do it.
    Does that scare you?

LOVER TWO:

    Not really. There's a waterfall
    of lovers like us.

LOVER ONE:

    You don't think we're all interchangeable
    do you?

LOVER TWO:

    I don't know.
    Maybe.

LOVER ONE:

    You mean one consciousness
    might as well be another?

LOVER TWO [*a little angry*]:
    I don't know!

[*The sound of dowels clacking together, and the stage goes black. Sycophant One and Sycophant Two enter in a pool of light. Sycophant One is pushing her bicycle and rings the bell.*]

SYCOPHANT ONE:
Hear ye! Hear ye!

[*A second pool of light comes up on a crowd of mice nearby. They peep occasionally.*]

MOUSE:
Peep. Peep. Peep. Peep.

ANOTHER MOUSE [*excitedly*]:
There's going to be a concert.
Where is Baby?

SYCOPHANT ONE:
There has been a tragedy in the life of Josephine.
Her pain is driving her to
greater intensity of song.
We cannot tell
you what her
sorrow is
but she is bereft.
It is a pain of loss.
She has lost someone.

SYCOPHANT TWO [*reading from a scroll*]:
Not only has she suffered loss
but she is exhausted from both
singing and her daily labor.
Unselfishly
she wishes only to please
you
in her
greatest pain.
Her sorrow in the beauty
of her songs may give support

94

to the tribe . . .
                   But . . .

[*He puts the scroll away and continues.*]

. . . she
must give in
to her pain and to her duties.
She
only wishes to bring you
the highest and the finest
so
rather than dilute her song
Josephine
will sing in the future
—till her wish is granted
by the judges—
she will sing
in the future
without grace
notes
in her
song.
There will be no grace notes.

[*He looks at the scroll again.*]

Her song will be unadorned.
No grace notes.

[*Sycophant One rings her bicycle bell. Josephine is drawn in by several mice. She is on a wagon with an elevated platform. She is in full splendor. Light beams from her. She begins to sing with her arms spread wide and ecstatic. Midway through the song she swoons at the beauty of it. Often as she sings she must clutch at her heart in ecstasy. Her torso swells and palpitates as she sings. She purses her lips and rolls her eyes. The song is flat and not rhythmic. Josephine's voice often wavers from the strain. The effect,*

*however, is ecstatic and beautiful and hints at moments
of what is wild. There are occasional drumbeats.*]

JOSEPHINE [*singing*]:
      Peep. Peep. Peep. Peep. Peep.
      Pipe. Peep. Peep. Peep. Pipe.
  Pipe. Peep. Pipe. Peep. Pipe. Peep.
      Peep. Peep. Peep. Peep. Peep.
      Peep. Peep. Peep. Peep. Peep.
      Peep. Peep. Peep. Peep. Peep.
      Peep. Peep. Peep. Peep. Peep.
  Pipe. Peep. Pipe. Peep. Pipe. Peep.
  Peep. Peep. Peep. Peep. Pipe. Pipe.
      Pipe. Peep. Pipe. Peep.
      Peep. Peep. Peep. Peep. Peep.
      Peep. Peep. Peep. Peep. Peep.
      Peep. Peep. Peep. Peep. Peep.
              Pipe. Peep.
              Peep. Peep.
              Pipe. Pipe.
    Peep. Peep. Peep. Peep.
    Peep. Peep. Peep. Peep.
    Peep. Peep. Peep. Peep.
    Peep. Peep. Peep. Peep.
    Peep. Pipe. Peep. Pipe.
    Peep. Pipe. Peep. Pipe.
    Peep. Pipe. Peep. Pipe.
  Pipe. Peep. Pipe. Peep. Pipe. Peep.
        Peep. Peep. Peep.
        Peep. Peep. Peep.
        Peep. Peep. Peep.
          Peep. Pipe.
          Pipe. Peep.
          Peep. Peep.
  Peep. Peep. Peep. Peep. Peep.
  Peep. Peep. Peep. Peep. Peep.
  Peep. Peep. Peep. Peep. Peep.
            Peep.
        Peep. Peep.

[*The light is dimmed on Josephine. She faints onto the floor of the wagon. The wagon is drawn off stage by the sycophants. The light on Josephine goes black. Sycophant One's bike bell is heard as the wagon is drawn away. The crowd of mice stands appreciatively. Mouse A clacks a pair of dowels and speaks to Mouse B. Later they are joined in conversation by Mouse C and Mouse D.*]

MOUSE A:

That was certainly beautiful.

MOUSE B:

It was Josephine all right.

MOUSE A:

Did you notice anything different?

MOUSE B:

You mean about the grace notes?

MOUSE A:

Yes.

[*The crowd of mice, including A, B, C, and D, begins to walk in a large circle. The pool of light follows them.*]

MOUSE B:

Did I miss the grace notes?
That's what you're asking?

MOUSE A:

That's it.

MOUSE B:

I can't tell if there
are grace notes or not.

MOUSE A:

Her song sounded like
always?

MOUSE B:

As nearly as I can tell.
I'm not a specialist or anything.

MOUSE A:

That's what I thought too.
I couldn't tell any difference.

MOUSE B:

Better show than usual though
wasn't it?

MOUSE A:

Yes. She seems to be more
emotional to make up for the missing
grace
notes.

MOUSE B:

That's what
I
thought.

MOUSE C:

Shhhh!

MOUSE D:

Be quiet.

MOUSE A:

Nothing wrong with a discussion
of artistry.

MOUSE D:

Time is passing.

MOUSE A:

Remember when she used to do the tremolo notes?

MOUSE B:
           Yes. We called them staccato.

MOUSE A:
             You could hear those.

MOUSE B:
           Mmmmm-hmmmm . . .

MOUSE C:
              Shhhh.

MOUSE D:
             Time's passing.

MOUSE C:
              Shhhh.

MOUSE D:
             Well, not much.
             Just a little bit.

MOUSE C:
              Shhhhh.
        Peep.   Peep.   Peep.   Peep.

MOUSE A AND MOUSE B:
        Peep.   Peep.   Peep.   Peep.

[*Immediately in front of the crowd of mice a spotlight flashes on. In the spot is Josephine. She is in the wagon and poised to sing. Beside her are the sycophants. Sycophant One rings the bike bell. There is a faint drumbeat.*]

SYCOPHANT ONE [*addressing the crowd*]:
             In view of your great loss
              of the grace notes . . .

SYCOPHANT TWO:

> And in concern
> that you may take
> their absence
> as a punishment . . .

SYCOPHANT ONE [*continuing*]:

> . . . We have implored
> Josephine to
> sing again
> with the grace notes.
> Her sad grief in her loss
> should not extend our tribe's
> pain. Josephine
> is the extinguisher
> and palliator
> of our pains.

JOSEPHINE [*grandly to the crowd*]:

> **AND SO I SHALL NOT KEEP YOU**
> **FROM THIS DEEPENING**
> **OF**
> **YOUR**
> **CONSCIOUSNESS.**

MOUSE A:

> Hoooray!

MOUSE C:

> Sing!

MOUSE B:

> Give us the grace notes.

JOSEPHINE:

> With these grace notes
> all that you feel shall
> build new, deep,
> greater structures

100

with the simple
notes
of
song
—and you shall be uplifted.

SYCOPHANT ONE:
And Josephine shall tell
you of her vow.

JOSEPHINE:
I vow never to have a husband or a lover.
And though that
means you might
lose songs in my children,
I
make
my vow
of celibacy
so that all
the little energy
I
have
may go
to please you.

MOUSE A:
Yeah!

MOUSE B:
Hoooray!

MOUSE C:
That's a dreadful vow!

SYCOPHANT TWO:
And now . . .

101

SYCOPHANT ONE:

 . . . Josephine sings . . .

SYCOPHANT TWO:

 . . . And with the grace notes!

[*Josephine begins to sing the same song and exactly as before.*]

JOSEPHINE:

Peep. Peep. Peep. Peep. Peep.
Pipe. Peep. Peep. Peep. Pipe.
Pipe. Peep. Pipe. Peep. Pipe. Peep.
Peep. Peep. Peep. Peep. Peep.
Peep. Peep. Peep. Peep. Peep.
Peep. Peep. Peep. Peep. Peep.
Peep. Peep. Peep. Peep. Peep.
Pipe. Peep. Pipe. Peep. Pipe. Peep.
Peep. Peep. Peep. Peep. Pipe. Pipe.
Pipe. Peep. Pipe. Peep.
Peep. Peep. Peep. Peep. Peep.
Peep. Peep. Peep. Peep. Peep.
Peep. Peep. Peep. Peep. Peep.

[*Lover One and Lover Two burst into the light and throw themselves down in front of Josephine.*]

LOVER ONE:

Please! Josephine choose among us.

LOVER TWO:

Josephine, choose
him
or me.

LOVER ONE:

We must have you.

102

LOVER TWO:

We or many others.

JOSEPHINE:

NO!

LOVER ONE:

NO?

LOVER TWO [*a whisper*]:

She means it.

JOSEPHINE:

I will not be my body
unless
my
body
is
my songs
—and then you and every
other
have me!
That is my destiny!

SYCOPHANT TWO:

Hear! Hear!

JOSEPHINE:

But each protects himself
from
me
because
he
will not
free
me.
I
know

103

what I am
but
each one locks himself
at a certain level
—builds a wall upon
the plateau
to keep the perfect clouds away.
My songs
are rain
that falls
upon the corn
on mountain tops
but
each
listener
makes a tent
and lives within
a desert.
Free yourselves!
Free
me!

LOVER ONE:

Josephine! We're going to
do it.

[*He brandishes knife.*]

LOVER TWO:

Kill ourselves.

JOSEPHINE [*to crowd*]:

Free
me!

[*Josephine turns on her heel, and the light goes black on
her.*]

LOVER ONE [*kneeling, looking at the knife in his hand*]:
Hello, O Sharper-Than-the Tooth-of-Cat!
If I cannot
have
the body
of my
love
—the bulk of destiny—
then I'll do it.

[*To Lover Two*]

Help me.

LOVER TWO [*showing him how to kill themselves together*]:
We'll fall forward
together.

[*He holds his knife in front of himself at floor level.*]

LOVER ONE:
First: her name.

LOVER TWO [*crying out*]:
Josephine!

LOVER ONE:
Josephine!

LOVERS ONE AND TWO:
Josephine!

[*The lovers fall forward together on their knives. There is a lot of blood. They groan and cry out.*

[*The crowd cries out in shock or horror. The light goes out on the crowd.*

[*Ghost Mouse One, Ghost Mouse Two, and Ghost Mouse Three enter with their red ribbons fluttering and bells jingling. Their entry is a dance. They are angular in their movements of arms and legs.*]

GHOST MOUSE ONE [*finding the lovers*]:
Look, here's two more.

GHOST MOUSE THREE:
Ask them to join us!

GHOST MOUSE ONE [*shaking the lovers*]:
Hey! Hey! You guys!
You can still dance
and wander invisible,
untouchable, and icy
through the crowds.

GHOST MOUSE TWO:
Sure. Hey.

[*Jiggling the lovers.*]

LOVER ONE:
Look! Ghosts!

GHOST MOUSE TWO:
You're ghosts, too!

LOVER TWO:
Yeah. That's right.

[*To the other lover*]

Hey, let's join them.

LOVER ONE:
O.K.

GHOST MOUSE ONE:

O.K.

[*The lovers and ghosts all clasp hands and begin an angular dance accompanied by the bells of the ghosts.*

[*Light comes up on a group of mice being addressed by Sycophant One, who rings her bike bell occasionally for emphasis. As Sycophant One and Sycophant Two address the mice, the ghosts and lovers dance. They jostle the mice and make faces and gestures—but they are not seen or felt.*]

SYCOPHANT ONE:

Josephine is the sole exception
to your humdrum lives.
She
has a love of music
and she can transmit
it
to you.

[*She rings her bike bell.*]

SYCOPHANT TWO:

You could repay
her
for the joy
she brings you.
You gather in crowds
and drink in the beauty
of her songs.

[SYCOPHANT ONE *implores.*]

SYCOPHANT ONE:

Give her liberty from labor!

MOUSE IN THE CROWD:

Be quiet!

107

ANOTHER MOUSE:

> Shh! They've got a right
> to talk.

MOUSE:

> I don't want
> to hear them.
> Those weren't songs.
> Not real songs!

MOUSE:

> I saw you listening
> as quiet as any.

SYCOPHANT ONE:

> *You*
> *must*
> *control*
> *your*
> *fate!*

SYCOPHANT TWO:

> *And broaden*
> your minds!

MOUSE:

> Strange things are happening.

MOUSE:

> I've got the shivers.

MOUSE:

> I hear there was a wave
> of suicides.

MOUSE CHILD:
> Mama, what's a sui . . . sui . . . ?

MOTHER:

> Suicide, dear. Shhh!

MOUSE:

There's never been
an epidemic of suicides
before.

MOUSE:

My grandpa
knew a suicide.

MOUSE CHILD:

Mama, what's a . . .

MOTHER:

Shhh!

MOUSE:

Things have never been
so creepy.

MOUSE:

I like things calm and
ordinary . . .

MOUSE:

And as cheerful
as they can be.

[*The mouse ghosts rattle their bells.*

[*The stage goes to black.*

[*The spotlight comes up on Josephine. She is on a dais looking up at the judges. The judges are on a higher dais. They are in a spot also. There are drumbeats.*]

JOSEPHINE [*to the judges*]:
So, I have forsworn
all love
that might

109

be made
with my body
to preserve my
energies
for
song
to
bring
my
gift
to
our
people!

[*Pause*]

What more
can
you ask?

[*She bows her head.*]

Is there more
that I can
do?

[*Baby appears in a spot.*]

BABY [*to Josephine*]:
Remember
the moving
figures
of our love
on cliffs
of
joy
in rainstorms
lit by lightning
of our smiles

110

that crashed through
eternity
in thundering
evanescent
moments!

JOSEPHINE:

Where has Baby
gone?

[*Lover One steps into the light with Baby.*]

LOVER ONE:

And us! You never saw
us!

JUDGE:

So, Josephine . . .

[*He bangs his gavel.*]

Each
of us is a fountain
lit by moonbeams.
No
one
of
us
has much
more weight
than any other.
We are like countless roots
in fields of clover
or specks of dust that go spinning
in a sunbeam
—there's
a
flash
of

111

light
but
not much there.
Each of us is but a hair
upon a shaggy,
shambling
beast
we call the tribe
or people.
No
one of us stands
as a steeple
over any
others.
There are no gifts as rare
as any treasured thing
that anyone
can hold
within his hand.
You must understand
that we love you
—as
any
other
—as we would love your sister
and your brother
with
calm and solemn
joy
for all—for father
and for mother
and we
tell you:
NO.

[*Bangs gavel.*]

No, Josephine!

[*Bangs gavel.*]

NO!

[*Bangs gavel.*]

NO!

[*Bangs gavel.*]

NO!

[*Bangs gavel.*]

NO!

[*There is a swirl of musical instruments, and ghosts and lovers dance in a pool of light.*

[*Everything goes black.*

[*The Judge's voice says "NO," and a gavel bangs. There is a blare of an industrial work buzzer—then the gavel bangs—then the buzzer rings twice more.*

[*The Narrator's bell rings in the blackness. A spot comes up on the Narrator, who is standing on a rock ringing his bell. He stops. He looks thoughtfully at the bell. He rings it again.*]

NARRATOR:
     Josephine's our singer. She has the power
        of song. And if you hear her
    —if anyone does—then they become
        delirious—either all sighs
          or solemn silence.
    She is the sole exception among us.
      She has the love of music
    and she knows how to transmit it.

113

She was refused by the court
of judges. Now she has disappeared
just when she was supposed to sing.
She's vanished.
The crowd is hunting side-by-side
with her supporters
who are fearful.
This time she's clear gone.
She can't be cajoled into singing.
She's deserted us.
She calculates it to appear that
she is being driven on by her
destiny.
She has left us without her songs.
She controlled our hearts
—but not understanding us
she withdrew her power. But
then her song never
was more potent or meaningful
than the memory of it will be.
Her myth can only go downhill
as it whites-out in the endless
memory of our people
as Josephine joins the pantheon
of heroes,
our people's heroes, in our history.

[*There is a spot on a mouse in a Hercules costume—in lion skin and with club. He is slaying a dragon. The dragon is red and orange—it draws back its head and opens its fanged mouth to strike. Hercules mouse kills it with a blow of his club. Spotlight out. Hercules, and the following hero mice, are seen at the back of the stage. They are elevated and in brilliant grottoes—as if archetypes and radiant figures of the psyche and History.*]

[*When the spot on Hercules goes out the Narrator continues.*]

NARRATOR:
> In fact, Josephine will be a smaller
> and smaller episode
> in our eternal history.

[*There is a spot on another hero mouse. He is in a Viking helmet and cape. He holds a broadsword. He raises high a banner in the other hand and places it upon a mound of earth. There is the sound of seabirds and waves. Spot out.*]

NARRATOR [*continuing without taking notice of the heroes*]:
> Against our history,
> was Josephine's piping
> really—in fact—louder
> than the memory of it will be?

[*There is a spot on a mouse in a general's costume of the 18th century—and in a three-cornered plumed hat. He is on horseback and leading troops. The troops raise muskets in the tableau of a salute. Spot out.*]

NARRATOR:
> Or does everything pass?
> She has gone beyond
> the earthly sorrows she expected
> and like a chosen spirit
> she will happily lose herself
> in the endless throng of the heroes
> of our people . . .

[*Spotlights flicker back and forth on the Hercules, Viking, and General. The effect is beautiful and metaphysical. There is blackness except for the Narrator's spotlight.*]

NARRATOR:
> And soon she'll rise

115

to the ultimate redemption
—since we are no historians—
of being forgotten
like all her brothers.

[*Spotlight out on the Narrator. A spot comes up on Josephine on a raised dais. She is finishing her song and in an ecstatic posture. The lighting is beatific.*]

JOSEPHINE [*singing*]:
Peep. Peep. Peep. Peep. Peep.
Peep.
Peep. Peep.

[*The suicide lovers, and Baby, and the ghost mice appear and dance around Josephine. Blackness.*

[*The spotlight comes up on the Narrator. He rings his bell.*]

NARRATOR:
Thus our drama ends—
bringing myth and truth
to watchers and to friends.

[*Black. Curtain. End.*]

Some New Directions Paperbacks

Walter Abish, *Alphabetical Africa*. NDP375.
In the Future Perfect. NDP440.
Minds Meet. NDP387.
Ilangô Adigal, *Shilappadikaram*. NDP162.
Alain, *The Gods*. NDP382.
David Antin. *Talking at the Boundaries*. NDP388.
G. Apollinaire, *Selected Writings*.† NDP310.
Djuna Barnes, *Nightwood*. NDP98.
Charles Baudelaire, *Flowers of Evil*.† NDP71,
Paris Spleen. NDP294.
Martin Bax. *The Hospital Ship*. NDP402.
Gottfried Benn, *Primal Vision*.† NDP322.
Wolfgang Borchert, *The Man Outside*. NDP319.
Jorge Luis Borges, *Labyrinths*. NDP186.
Jean-François Bory, *Once Again*. NDP256.
E. Brock, *The Blocked Heart*. NDP399.
Here. Now. Always. NDP429.
Invisibility Is The Art of Survival. NDP342.
The Portraits & The Poses. NDP360.
The River and the Train. NDP478.
Buddha, *The Dhammapada*. NDP188.
Frederick Busch, *Domestic Particulars*. NDP413.
Manual Labor. NDP376.
Ernesto Cardenal, *Apocalypse & Other Poems*.
NDP441. *In Cuba*. NDP377.
Hayden Carruth, *For You*. NDP298.
From Snow and Rock, from Chaos. NDP349.
Louis-Ferdinand Céline,
Death on the Installment Plan. NDP330.
Guignol's Band. NDP278.
Journey to the End of the Night. NDP84.
Jean Cocteau, *The Holy Terrors*. NDP212.
The Infernal Machine. NDP235.
M. Cohen, *Monday Rhetoric*. NDP352.
Robert Coles. *Irony in the Mind's Life*, NDP459.
Cid Corman, *Livingdying*. NDP289.
Sun Rock Man. NDP318.
Gregory Corso, *Elegiac Feelings*. NDP299.
Happy Birthday of Death. NDP86.
Long Live Man. NDP127.
Robert Creeley, *Hello*. NDP451.
Edward Dahlberg, *Reader*. NDP246.
Because I Was Flesh. NDP227.
Osamu Dazai, *The Setting Sun*, NDP258.
No Longer Human. NDP357.
Coleman Dowell, *Mrs. October . . .* NDP368.
Too Much Flesh and Jabez. NDP447.
Robert Duncan, *Bending the Bow*. NDP255.
The Opening of the Field. NDP356.
Roots and Branches. NDP275.
Richard Eberhart, *Selected Poems*. NDP198.
E. F. Edinger. *Melville's Moby-Dick*. NDP460.
Russell Edson. *The Falling Sickness*. NDP389.
The Very Thing That Happens. NDP137.
Wm. Empson, *7 Types of Ambiguity*. NDP204.
Some Versions of Pastoral. NDP92.
Wm. Everson, *Man-Fate*. NDP369.
The Residual Years. NDP263.
Lawrence Ferlinghetti, *Her*. NDP88.
Back Roads to Far Places. NDP312.
A Coney Island of the Mind. NDP74.
The Mexican Night. NDP300.
Open Eye, Open Heart, NDP361.
Routines. NDP187.
The Secret Meaning of Things. NDP268.
Starting from San Francisco. NDP220.
Tyrannus Nix?. NDP288.
Who Are We Now? NDP425.
F. Scott Fitzgerald, *The Crack-up*. NDP54.
Robert Fitzgerald, *Spring Shade*. NDP311.
Gustave Flaubert, *Dictionary*. NDP230.
Gandhi, *Gandhi on Non-Violence*. NDP197.
Goethe, *Faust*, Part I. NDP70.
Allen Grossman. *The Woman on the Bridge*.
NDP473.
Albert J. Guerard, *Thomas Hardy*. NDP185.
John Hawkes, *The Beetle Leg*. NDP239.
The Blood Oranges. NDP338.
The Cannibal. NDP123.
Death Sleep & The Traveler. NDP393.
The Innocent Party. NDP238.
John Hawkes Symposium. NDP446.

The Lime Twig. NDP95.
Lunar Landscapes. NDP274.
The Owl. NDP443.
Second Skin. NDP146.
Travesty. NDP430.
A. Hayes, *A Wreath of Christmas Poems*.
NDP347.
H.D., *End to Torment*. NDP476.
Helen in Egypt. NDP380.
Hermetic Definition NDP343.
Trilogy. NDP362.
Robert E. Helbling, *Heinrich von Kleist*, NDP390.
Hermann Hesse, *Siddhartha*. NDP65.
C. Isherwood, *All the Conspirators*. NDP480.
The Berlin Stories. NDP134.
Lions and Shadows, NDP435.
Philippe Jaccottet, *Seedtime*. NDP428.
Alfred Jarry, *The Supermale*. NDP426.
Ubu Roi, NDP105.
Robinson Jeffers, *Cawdor and Meda*. NDP293.
James Joyce, *Stephen Hero*. NDP133.
James Joyce/Finnegans Wake. NDP331.
Franz Kafka, *Amerika*. NDP117.
Bob Kaufman,
Solitudes Crowded with Loneliness. NDP199.
Hugh Kenner, *Wyndham Lewis*. NDP167.
Kenyon Critics, *G. M. Hopkins*. NDP355.
H. von Kleist. *Prince Friedrich of Homburg*.
NDP462.
P. Lai, *Great Sanskrit Plays*. NDP142.
Tommaso Landolfi,
Gogol's Wife and Other Stories. NDP155.
Lautréamont, *Maldoror*. NDP207.
Irving Layton, *Selected Poems*. NDP431.
Denise Levertov, *Collected Earlier Poems*.
NDP475.
Footprints. NDP344.
The Freeing of the Dust. NDP401.
The Jacob's Ladder. NDP112.
Life in the Forest. NDP461.
O Taste and See. NDP149.
The Poet in the World. NDP363.
Relearning the Alphabet. NDP290.
The Sorrow Dance. NDP222.
To Stay Alive. NDP325.
In Her Own Province. NDP481.
Harry Levin, *James Joyce*. NDP87.
Enrique Lihn, *The Dark Room*.† NDP452.
García Lorca, *Five Plays*. NDP232.
Selected Poems.† NDP114.
Three Tragedies. NDP52.
Michael McClure, *Gorf*. NDP416.
Antechamber. NDP455.
Jaguar Skies. NDP400.
September Blackberries. NDP370.
Carson McCullers, *The Member of the
Wedding*. (Playscript) NDP153.
Thomas Merton, *Asian Journal*. NDP394.
Gandhi on Non-Violence. NDP197.
My Argument with the Gestapo. NDP403.
New Seeds of Contemplation. NDP337.
Raids on the Unspeakable. NDP213.
Selected Poems. NDP85.
The Way of Chuang Tzu. NDP2776.
The Wisdom of the Desert. NDP295.
Zen and the Birds of Appetite. NDP261.
Henry Miller, *The Air-Conditioned Nightmare*.
NDP302.
Big Sur & The Oranges. NDP161.
The Books in My Life. NDP280.
The Colossus of Maroussi. NDP75.
The Cosmological Eye. NDP109.
Henry Miller on Writing. NDP151.
The Henry Miller Reader. NDP269.
Just Wild About Harry. NDP479.
The Smile at the Foot of the Ladder. NDP386.
Stand Still Like the Hummingbird. NDP236.
The Time of the Assassins. NDP115.
The Wisdom of the Heart. NDP94.
Y. Mishima, *Confessions of a Mask*. NDP253.
Death in Midsummer. NDP215.
Eugenio Montale, *New Poems*. NDP410.
Selected Poems.† NDP193.
Vladimir Nabokov, *Nikolai Gogol*. NDP78.
Laughter in the Dark. NDP470.

The Real Life of Sebastian Knight. NDP432.
P. Neruda, *The Captain's Verses.*† NDP345.
  Residence on Earth.† NDP340.
New Directions in Prose & Poetry (Anthology).
  Available from #17 forward. #38, Spring 1979.
Robert Nichols, *Arrival.* NDP437.
  Garh City. NDP450.
  Harditts in Sawna. NDP470.
Charles Olson, *Selected Writings.* NDP231.
Toby Olson. *The Life of Jesus.* NDP417.
George Oppen, *Collected Poems.* NDP418.
Wilfred Owen, *Collected Poems.* NDP210.
Nicanor Parra, *Emergency Poems.*† NDP333.
  Poems and Antipoems.† NDP242.
Boris Pasternak, *Safe Conduct.* NDP77.
Kenneth Patchen, *Aflame and Afun.* NDP292.
  Because It Is. NDP83.
  But Even So. NDP265.
  Collected Poems. NDP284.
  Doubleheader. NDP211.
  Hallelujah Anyway. NDP219.
  In Quest of Candlelighters. NDP334.
  The Journal of Albion Moonlight. NDP99.
  Memoirs of a Shy Pornographer. NDP205.
  Selected Poems. NDP160.
  Wonderings. NDP320.
Octavio Paz, *Configurations.*† NDP303.
  Eagle or Sun?† NDP422.
  Early Poems.† NDP354.
Plays for a New Theater. (Anth.) NDP216.
J. A. Porter, *Eelgrass.* NDP438.
Ezra Pound, *ABC of Reading.* NDP89.
  Classic Noh Theatre of Japan. NDP79.
  Confucius. NDP285.
  Confucius to Cummings. (Anth.) NDP126.
  Gaudier Brzeska. NDP372.
  Guide to Kulchur. NDP257.
  Literary Essays. NDP250.
  Love Poems of Ancient Egypt. NDP178.
  Pavannes and Divagations. NDP397.
  Pound/Joyce. NDP296.
  Selected Cantos. NDP304.
  Selected Letters 1907-1941. NDP317.
  Selected Poems. NDP66.
  Selected Prose 1909-1965. NDP396.
  The Spirit of Romance. NDP266.
  Translations.† (Enlarged Edition) NDP145.
James Purdy, *Children Is All.* NDP327.
Raymond Queneau, *The Bark Tree.* NDP314.
  The Flight of Icarus. NDP358.
  The Sunday of Life. NDP433.
Mary de Rachewiltz, *Ezra Pound.* NDP405.
M. Randall, *Part of the Solution.* NDP350.
John Crove Ransom, *Beating the Bushes.*
  NDP324.
Raja Rao, *Kanthapura.* NDP224.
Herbert Read, *The Green Child.* NDP208.
P. Reverdy, *Selected Poems.*† NDP346.
Kenneth Rexroth, *Beyond the Mountains.*
  NDP384.
  Collected Longer Poems. NDP309.
  Collected Shorter Poems. NDP243.
  New Poems. NDP383.
  100 More Poems from the Chinese. NDP308.
  100 More Poems from the Japanese. NDP420.
  100 Poems from the Chinese. NDP192.
  100 Poems from the Japanese.† NDP147.
Rainer Maria Rilke, *Poems from*
  The Book of Hours. NDP408.
  Possibility of Being. NDP436.
  Where Silence Reigns. (Prose). NDP464.
Arthur Rimbaud, *Illuminations.*† NDP56.
  Season in Hell & Drunken Boat.† NDP97.
Edouard Roditi, *Delights of Turkey.* NDP445.
Selden Rodman, *Tongues of Fallen Angels.*
  NDP373.
Jerome Rothenberg, *Poems for the Game*
  of Silence. NRP406.
  Poland/1931. NDP379.
  Seneca Journal. NDP448.
Saikaku Ihara, *The Life of an Amorous*
  Woman. NDP270.

Saigyo. *Mirror for the Moon.*† NDP465.
St. John of the Cross, *Poems.*† NDP341.
Jean-Paul Sartre, *Baudelaire.* NDP233.
  Nausea. NDP82.
  The Wall (*Intimacy*). NDP272.
Delmore Schwartz, *Selected Poems.* NDP241.
  In Dreams Begin Responsibilities. NDP454.
Kazuko Shiraishi, *Seasons of Sacred Lust.*
  NDP453.
Stevie Smith, *Selected Poems,* NDP159.
Gary Snyder, *The Back Country.* NDP249.
  Earth House Hold. NDP267.
  Myths and Texts. NDP457.
  Regarding Wave. NDP306.
  Turtle Island. NDP381.
Gilbert Sorrentino, *Splendide-Hôtel.* NDP364.
Enid Starkie, *Rimbaud.* NDP254.
Stendhal, *The Telegraph.* NDP108.
Jules Supervielle, *Selected Writings.*† NDP209.
W. Sutton, *American Free Verse.* NDP351.
Nathaniel Tarn, *Lyrics...Bride of God.* NDP391.
Dylan Thomas, *Adventures in the Skin Trade.*
  NDP183.
  A Child's Christmas in Wales. NDP181.
  Collected Poems 1934-1952. NDP316.
  The Doctor and the Devils. NDP297.
  Portrait of the Artist as a Young Dog.
  NDP51.
  Quite Early One Morning. NDP90.
  Under Milk Wood. NDP73.
Martin Turnell, *Art of French Fiction.* NDP251.
  Baudelaire. NDP336.
  Rise of the French Novel. NDP474.
Paul Valéry, *Selected Writings.*† NDP184.
P. Van Ostaijen, *Feasts of Fear & Agony.*
  NDP411.
Elio Vittorini, *A Vittorini Omnibus.* NDP366.
  Women of Messina. NDP365.
Vernon Watkins, *Selected Poems.* NDP221.
Nathanael West, *Miss Lonelyhearts &*
  Day of the Locust. NDP125.
J. Williams, *An Ear in Bartram's Tree.* NDP335.
Tennessee Williams, *Camino Real,* NDP301.
  Cat on a Hot Tin Roof. NDP398.
  Dragon Country. NDP287.
  Eight Mortal Ladies Possessed, NDP374.
  The Glass Menagerie. NDP218.
  Hard Candy. NDP225.
  In the Winter of Cities. NDP154.
  One Arm & Other Stories. NDP237.
  The Roman Spring of Mrs. Stone. NDP271.
  Small Craft Warnings. NDP348.
  Sweet Bird of Youth. NDP409.
  Twenty-Seven Wagons Full of Cotton. NDP217.
  Vieux Carré. NDP482.
  Where I Live, NDP468.
William Carlos Williams.
  The Autobiography. NDP223.
  The Build-up. NDP259.
  Embodiment of Knowledge. NDP434.
  The Farmers' Daughters. NDP106.
  I Wanted to Write a Poem. NDP469.
  Imaginations. NDP329.
  In the American Grain. NDP53.
  In the Money. NDP240.
  Paterson. Complete. NDP152.
  Pictures from Brueghel. NDP118.
  The Selected Essays. NDP273.
  Selected Poems. NDP131.
  A Voyage to Pagany. NDP307.
  White Mule. NDP226.
  W. C. Williams Reader. NDP282.
Yvor Winters, *E. A. Robinson.* NDP326.
Wisdom Books: *Ancient Egyptians,* NDP467;
  Wisdom of the Desert, NDP295; *Early*
  Buddhists, NDP444; *English Mystics,* NDP466;
  Forest (Hindu), NDP414; *Jewish Mystics,*
  NDP423; *Spanish Mystics,* NDP442; *Sufi,*
  NDP424; *Zen Masters,* NDP415.

Complete descriptive catalog available free on request from
New Directions, 80 Eighth Avenue, New York 10011   † Bilingual